100 IRONM
IN 100 [

]

— *From the Transcript of the Ed Mylett Show*

Announcer (00:00:07):

This is the Ed Mylett Show.

Ed Mylett (00:00:16):

Hey, welcome back to the show, everybody. Hey, have you ever thought about running a marathon? Because I've thought about it. I'm like, there's a, there's an Ironman in Coeur d'Alene where I spent my summers, just the marathon part of it. I was like, that's bananas 26 miles, you know? And have you ever thought about doing that, or have you ever watched one of these Ironmen and gone, "I'm going to do that someday"?

By the way, it's about a two and a half-mile swim, 112 miles on a bike, 26-mile run. That's kind of what an iron-length triathlon is. I want you to imagine doing one of those. Then I want you to imagine getting up the next day and doing it again.

Can you imagine back-to-back days? Then I want you to contemplate thinking about doing it 30 freaking days in a row. You got that? How about 50 days in a row? How about 100 days in a row? Get your mind around that. Okay.

That would be one of the great all-time athletic endurance feats in the history of the world, and simultaneously one of the great mental toughness and resiliency feats of all time. Guess what? I got the dude here today, who did it. A hundred in a row in 100 days. His name is Iron Cowboy. James Lawrence. Welcome to the program, brother.

James Lawrence (00:01:41):

Hey, Ed, man. I, I've got to tell ya. I'm going to try to keep it together as we talk. Um, obviously just came off of an insanely emotional journey physically, mentally, spiritually. But I got to tell you, huge, huge love, adoration and respect for you.

You may have single-handedly and unknowingly got me through this quarter of a year challenge because, um, during the 112-mile bike ride every day, um, I would tee you up, man. And, um, you're I don't know if it was, um, just how soothing your voice was, but like, I was like, I got to the point where I got through all of it and then I would have to wait because I caught up and I'd have to wait until the next one dropped. And I was always so, excited when it did.

And so, I just wanted to say, man, thank you so, much for being part of my journey, not knowing you were part of my journey. Um, so, yeah, I just want to thank you.

Ed Mylett (00:02:38):

I did see a post from one of your daughters that had said that you were listening to the show during it, it makes me choked up to think it for two reasons. Number one, it's an honor to have been a speck in the sand of the beach of what you did. Number two, it's as close as I'm ever going to get to doing what you did. That's at least that was at least I was in your ears, brother.

James Lawrence (00:02:55):

You were out there every day with me, brother.

Ed Mylett (00:02:57):

Hey, everybody. So, we're going to talk today about all kinds of stuff, obviously, you know, resistant, quitting, overcoming fear, overcoming pain, mental toughness. Honestly, I, if you've listened to that introduction, everybody, it would sound like this is easy, but it's not. And then also he did it for underground railroad, you know, raising money. There was a reason behind there's so, many things, but I want to go back just because you would think you do this and even looking at you, you look like a wrestler.

I think visually when I look at you look like a wrestler, I'm thinking this dude, when I you know, we've been following each other for a while, I'm going to see this guy. He's probably 6'3, you know, real long legs, super lean. He's probably got some athletic advantage. Because everybody wants a discount success. Right? I've probably got some.

Then I started reading on it. Scott was a high school wrestler, like lost about every match his freshman year. So, there was no gift there. Kind of tried to play a little professional golf, you know, that didn't work out, but visually it's not like you have some athletic gift to be doing this. Right. So, what, what was the, what was the catalyst to get you to go? I'm going to do some endurance sports. What made you do that?

James Lawrence (00:04:03):

It's interesting. I mean, everybody has a start to their journey. Right? And, um, like you said, I grew up wrestling. I loved it. I gravitate towards individual sports. because like not realizing it, but looking back on what I've done, I did wrestling and then golf and then triathlon. And they're all individual sports because I love that if I win or I lose it's my fault. And I love that accountability of it.

And man, I, like you said, I got, I got tooled, um, beyond comprehension when I first started wrestling. But then I went undefeated my senior year and went on to represent Canada, which is where I grew up. Um, and then I got married and uh, found my beautiful bride. And we've got five kids just celebrated 20 years of marriage. but back in the day, um, she was into running and she was like, "Hey, let's go do this four-miles fun run."

And I'm like, what are you talking about? Nobody says fun. And have you ever seen a runner? Like going down the road, smiling? No, it's impossible. Like stop talking. And she was like, just come do it. It'll be fun. I'm like, it's Thanksgiving. I'm like, okay, I'll be the good husband. I'll go support my wife. And, um, dude, I distinctly remember like, I'm like my heart's pounding my lungs feel like they're going to explode.

And I look over and these beautiful women just pushing their kids in strollers, laughing and talking, just blowing by me. And I'm like, what the hell? Like, I'm a physical specimen. Like what is going on? That this is happening in my life right now. And so, it, it allowed me to sit back and do kind of like a mini audit on where I was physically in my life.

And I had some situational depression, and I was a new father of these two beautiful girls. And I just was like trying to figure out my place. And uh, and Sonny comes out to me. It was Thanksgiving looks right at me and she's like, dude, you are pathetic. And I was just like, whoa, what are we talking about here? And she's like, I just, I just signed you up for the Salt Lake City marathon. Um, figure it out."

And I was like a marathon. I'm like, what's that? How far are we talking here? And she's like, "Well, it's 26.2 miles and it's in four months. And, and I, and I just like, it just rocked me and I went and did the marathon and I actually hated it. Funny story. The MMA fights were in town. I'm a huge MMA fan. They were in town that night and I went to the stadium in Salt Lake City.

I sat down in my chair and I'm like, I'm. I had this terrible marathon experience. I'm just going to sit here and watch the show. Well, four hours go by and I go to stand up to go home. And I can't, and I looked down and my knees had swollen up to the size of cantaloupes and I could not stand up out of my chair.

And so, now picture the much of a list of environments and I have to get wheelchaired out of this to my car and eat just the big, like the entire humble pie I had eat the whole thing, not a piece, the whole thing. And I got home and I was just like f*** running and endurance sports. Like this is so, stupid. I'm like, I'm a wrestler, I'm a fighter. I'm a guy that goes to the weight room and does the weights. I don't care. Then I woke up the next morning and I went, I can do that better.

And I said, I am not going to allow that moment to define who I am. And then I, over time I learned, because you hear all the time, I don't run, I've got bad knees. And I was, I was that guy. I was like, I've got bad knees. It's obvious I got bad knees. I must've been from all the wrestling and I'm not a runner.

And then I learned over educated myself, and whatnot. I don't have bad knees, because of running, I have bad knees because I don't run. And I started to go down this journey of endurance and I found the love for cycling. And I got into the tour de France and watching it. And I had a friend that did sprint triathlon, which is the short version.

And I just fell in love. I had to teach myself how to swim and buy a bike. And I just fell in love with the, the, the diversity of training. and I didn't look like everybody else. Right? Like I was, I carry more muscle. And I, I remember early on, I went to Iron Man, um, Ironman, Arizona, and I was spectating.

And I have no idea what his name is, but I watched the fourth place professional. He was either fourth or third come across the line. And this dude looked like you. I mean, he was yoked. And I was like, okay, you can look like an athlete and still have success in this, in this game. And so, then I just, my passion is truly like lifting and, and, and that's where, that's where my, I started in wrestling and fighting and all that.

And so, when I saw that, I was like, okay, I might be able to be successful in this sport. And I just fell in love with the diversity of it and the training. And then what I learned was a lot of this is mental. And going back to my roots was, was triathlon. I mean was wrestling. And again, if I win or I lose, it's my fault. And I loved that.

And so, I just started to implement, um, the mental side of stuff and the nutrition side of stuff. And it just became this like big challenge for me. And over time it just escalated. And I would try one thing and gain experience. And, and I totally long story, but we lost everything in the economy. I used to own a mortgage company and all of these things happen.

And I remember doing my first iron man triathlon. And, um, I just fell in love with it. It was hard to have the perfect race. And again, it was like, I can do better. I can do better. I can do better. And you just keep going back to the drawing board, trying to do better.

And I started working for a charity and it was a charity in Africa. And we ended up breaking the world record for the most half Ironmans done in a year. And it was so, cool because it was the hardest thing I could think of. It totally pushed me physically and mentally.

And, and as you know, the number one question that a lot of people get that a lot of people ask or want to know in today's day and age is like, how do I become more mentally tough? It's like, how? And I'm like, well, you have to show up. And it's only through experience that you can become more mentally tough.

And what I've experienced over my career is like, when you're, when you set a goal, it should be the most intimidating, scary, but exciting goal that you've ever set for yourself. And as you work towards it, and then when you're in the middle of it, you say to yourself, this is the hardest thing I've ever done. And then you accomplish it. And you're like, ah, yes, I did that.

And now I have knowledge and experience and you look back at what was the hardest thing, and you say, I can do better. Yeah. And now you've gained, you've gained confidence and knowledge because you decided to show up and not quit. And only then can you now conceptualize the next big goal.

Because I didn't wake up and just go, you know what? Life is hard and I don't have much experience, but I'm going to go do conquer 100. Right? You don't, you don't go from there to there. And if you, I do, I guarantee you you're going to fail, right? Because one, you don't respect the goal and you haven't endured the process to where you gain knowledge and experience.

And so, the, that half Ironman led me to the full Ironman world record that led me to the consecutive two, where I then believed that I was capable physically immensely to do a quarter of a year of 100 consecutive full distance tries, which is unreal, quartz, sports, endurance history.

Ed Mylett (00:11:51):

I want to unpack that for a minute. So, I wonder, want to catch this because you've got a dream. Maybe you want to maybe like, maybe you're sitting here going, look, I don't know what my big thing is yet. What'd you just unpack two things because he said to him, you know, in one bunch, one, this is the guy that runs struggles through his first four-mile deal. Right. Gets wheeled out of the arena. Right. Which is incredible.

Like after the first, the first big one you did then to think that this is really, this came on the heels of catastrophe in your life, which was your mortgage business failing. Right? I mean, I want everyone understand this through one of the most difficult times in this man's life was really born this new adventure slash challenge in his life.

This did not come like in, you know, spring season of his life. It came in wintertime. And can you go back to that just for a minute? I mean, were you, did this give you some kind of like a release, like, hey, this is something maybe I can prove myself in again, like you said, I loved it. Did you love the actual sweating in the, your gas by the end of it? Or did you love the challenge of the whole thing? Because you had kind of had this business setback.

James Lawrence (00:12:56):

I love the challenge of the whole thing, and I want to congratulate anybody right now that is at rock bottom. Um, because if you choose to get up and fight your life is going to be so, spectacular. And, and to me, the best place that I could've ever been was rock bottom, because it gave me an opportunity to claw back and fight and take back what was mine, improve who I was. And so, I just want to like, look, if you're struggling right now and you feel like there's no way out, you're exactly where you need to be. And if you can wake up and say, look, I'm just going to win today. And you don't, you, don't got to get all the way there, but if you just show up and, and, and, and have intent with what you're doing, dude, I'm so, excited for you because that's where I was.

And I'm telling you, I'm, I'm living the life of my dreams right now. And I, I have the relationship of my dreams. I've got five kids of my dreams, and none of it would have happened without the lessons and the destruction and everything that I experienced. And so, I just want to congratulate anybody listening that if you're in the thick of it and you feel like there's no way out, congratulations, because if you choose to show up with intent every single day, uh, you're going to take your life back and you can, because I did. And I'm nobody,

Ed Mylett (00:14:28):

Wouldn't it be cool. If there was a pocket-sized guy that could help you sleep focus, act be better. There actually is. It's called Headspace. I use it daily Headspace as your daily dose of mindfulness in the form of a guided meditations in an easy-to-use app. It's one of the only meditation apps advancing the field of mindfulness and meditation through clinically validated research. So, whatever the situation is, really Headspace can help you.

If you're overwhelmed, it has a three-minute SOS meditation for you. You need some help falling asleep. It's got wind down sessions that I use almost every single night. And I swear by them. It's just awesome. The main thing I've used Headspace for is sleeping at night, but for many years prior to that, I used it in the morning for my meditations as well. You can use it for both. It's like 60 million downloads. It's the real deal. So, you deserve to feel happier, and Headspace makes meditation completely simple. So, go to headspace.com/mylett that's headspace.com/mylett for a free one-month trial with access to headspaces full library of meditations. For every situation you're going to love it. This is the best deal offered anywhere right now, headspace.com/mylett. Let's get back at it.

Ed Mylett (00:15:36):

That's awesome. You know, bro, that's one of those I just sit and a base in that for a minute. It made me think, by the way, you can tell he's obviously one of the best speakers in the country too. And his book redefined impossible. The honor cowboy redefining possible is really what you did. You redefine what was possible to write, but I've sat at those iron mans. Cause I lived in Coeur d'Alene. So, I started an actual iron man, one of the trademark ones, and I don't go to watch the pros finish. I've gone. I like to go at nighttime. It's usually raining and you're watching a 82 year old priest finish by the end of the night, right? Or a guy with a prosthetic leg or a lady who's just survived stage four cancer. And what happens to you when you watch something like that?

And then what you've done is some level that's just beyond comprehension almost is that I weep and everyone's crying. And I, after about six years of doing this, my kids are like dad cries once a year. You know, it's watching these beautiful souls make something that seemed impossible possible. And I concluded that we're all crying because we know this courage, this mental toughness, this incredible thing, these people are displaying. We also have inside us and we're not utilizing. And that's why it's a tear. It's not laughter it's a tear because I know it's tears of joy, but it's also tears of personal reflection. And when I was watching you finish this thing, I was reflecting. It's amazing. You're listening to some of my stuff, but I was, I was reflecting me. I just literally lost my breath. Say I was reflecting. Like, what am I capable of?

What, what's the last massive challenge I've taken on in my life? And I'm curious for you, I want to go through it because I think there's metaphors everywhere. So, he's, by the way, the reason I started with 30 and 50 as he's done that. And then when you did the 50 and 50, I'm like, bro, like you're out of your mind. Right. And then to go do the Cocker 100, but I'm reading about both, you know, both of those last two, it's inspiring. Right? But this time like day five, your shin start exploding, right? Like you're on day five. Talk, talk us through that. Did you think of quitting then? So,

James Lawrence (00:17:41):

So, two really cool things happened. Um, that took me a little bit of time to realize, um, I went into it, um, knowing that you can't train for 100 consecutive, you have to adapt and evolve along the way. And I knew, look, the first 15 and 20 of these are going to be hell, because you've got to get to the point where you're broken physically, mentally, and then push through that. And that's where everybody quits. And if I can push through that, my body's going to adapt and evolve and it's going to become the new normal everybody.

Ed Mylett (00:18:12):

I want you to write this down, pull over, adapt and evolve. That's in your business, that's in your family, that's in your fitness. That's, that's the key. Go ahead. Keep going.

James Lawrence (00:18:19):

Yeah. And so, when I went into it with, an ankle problem that I didn't tell anybody about, um, and it immediately exploded into my shin to where we developed a stress fracture in the bone and super long story, but a miracle happened. We ended up getting a carbon plated chin sprung, a brace that allowed, allowed the, the allowed us to offload the shin and continue on to heal that stress fracture by doing the marathon portion every single day, it was a Mo it was a total miracle, but a complete Testament to me that you give your body the tools and assets that it needs to recover. It can still do so, under stress. And that was amazing to me to watch the body heal like that. Now the, the shin and the, and the imbalance that created a hip problem became so, painful some of my worst days.

Um, I don't remember them, but we have the video footage where I would be, trying to move and the pain would get to a point that I could no longer manage it. And I would black out. And my, my, we called them the wing man. My wingman would catch me, I'd come back to, and he would do a ten second countdown and then say, here we go. And we would repeat that until I got to the I'm going to be emotional, but until I got to the finish line that night, and, um, it, again, it's just a Testament to how powerful the mind is now. I, I was angry because, um, I wanted to showcase how strong our team was mentally and physically. And I wanted to make the hundred look easy. I believed we could do that. Um, and I was angry that I couldn't run. And then I was forced to walk.

Hmm. And it turned out to be the biggest blessing of the entire campaign. Um, my, my, um, my pain and discomfort forced me to walk. And every single day we had people from around the country fly in and locals to support us. And without fail, they said, I'm so, grateful. You're walking because I wouldn't have been able to join you if you, if you weren't walking. And, uh, and I was hard on myself because I was like, look, I'm an athlete. I want to destroy this.

And, um, as, as I, as I got deeper into it, I was like, I'm so, grateful for this injury. I'm so, grateful. I'm walking. And, and my, my pain has turned into a blessing that other people can join and have an experience. And every single day, somebody did their first 10 K with me or their first marathon or their first full distance, or their first hungry, 100-mile bike ride. And every single day I got to experience somebody else's first and it was humbling. And it was, um, yeah, humbling. Wow.

Ed Mylett (00:21:49):

I mean, by the end of this, you guys, a couple of hundred people riding the cyclists with them and you, I actually, for you am grateful that it didn't look easy because I think you connected, at least with me watching you struggle, I'm on Instagram every night, watching these videos when it was happening. Like there were literally times for me watching you, like I'm in tears, like not wondering the next day, just, but it's one of the most, I don't even like to say one of the most, because when I say that, then I have to think of something that I think is more, it's just insanely inspiring. And I can't think of something mentally or physically I've ever seen close to this because of the adversity, because of all the people that got caught up in it with you also though, there's an Eller element of this that, you know, this idea of adapting maps is so, glad that you said that for everybody's sake, but I I'm curious of all of them, but one your time you did the 50 or this time, was there a moment where you're like, I'm out, I'm going to TA like you're literally blacking out.

Right. So, that's insane to me, but was there a time when you just consciously went I'm in too much pain I'm in too much. Cause guys, these are icy roads. Snowy. Sometimes you mentioned shin issues on a snowy ice. Oh my gosh. Like, like, was there a point or are there lots of points where you're like, I'm out, but is there one particular bro where you're like, no, no. Like this time I'm really out.

James Lawrence (00:23:22):

So, um, my team is world-class, um, and, and there's, there's the core four of us. It's my wife, sunny Jo. Um, and then the two wing men, Casey and Aaron, and they were, they were the four of us thick and thin through the 50. And then, and then I brought those boys back on for the 100 and they played massive roles and

Sonny's obviously the head of this, this entire thing. Um, and we, we just know from experience that, um, it's okay to feel. It's not okay to quit. It's okay to problem solve. It's not okay to quit and it, and it's okay to, and I think that's what a lot of people don't do, especially men is they don't allow themselves to feel them processed us before they hunker down and keep going. Um, at no point in time was ever any of us saying, you know, we're quit and we gotta be talked back into it.

But every single one of us had moments where we just needed to cry, to feel, uh, be, um, supported to where we said, okay, I've had my two minutes. I'm not going to dwell on it. We're going to, we're going to quickly turn this around and we're going to get back to work. And that's the reason the four of us are so, strong together because all four of us have that mindset. And I will tell you this, the closest that I ever came to even considering it was somewhere between 15 and 20, um, where we were at the peak of that pain, where I had, a couple of days where I was blacking out. I don't remember portions of it. And I remember standing in the shower and I kind of just shrugged my shoulders, at Sonny. And I said, I don't know how many more days I can manage the pain at that level, because when you've got 85 more days to go, that is so, it's so, daunting when you're broken you, it's hard to conceptualize what it's like, and I'll never forget.

She said, she said, um, you're done today, and you don't have to do anything else. And all you have to do is now trust in the team, get out of the shower, go lay on the table and let them take care of you. And then we will face whatever comes tomorrow together. Gosh. And I think that's what a lot of people don't do is, is you've, you've got this today's mentality of the people that do decide to show up that it's like, I gotta go in all the time. I got to go all in all the time. Uh, I got to hurt more than he does, and they don't take two seconds to run reset mentally. And, and I can't tell you how important that was. And the valuable lesson that I learned was you've done enough today to take two seconds and reset. And as soon as I got into that rhythm, knowing, and, and again, it takes, it takes putting the right team together and then it takes letting go and trusting the team that you have put together to do their job, to do their part.

And that's hard too, as a, as a man to let go of like control of every piece of that puzzle and to go, I, I surrender, and I trust you to do your part. And it's hard to find good people nowadays that are willing to do their part. Um, and, and I have that team. And so, when Sonny said, you've, you've done enough today. And I think that's so, important because we go through life and I think we're so, hard on ourselves. We see ourselves differently. And how many, how many times in our lives on our journeys, do we take a minute and say, you're enough. You've done enough. And I think it's so, important, especially as men to be, to be vulnerable. And just say, I've done enough today. I'm going to take on tomorrow. When tomorrow comes.

Ed Mylett (00:27:18):

Very surprised to hear you say it yet. It resonates with me as complete truth. Just one of the biggest badass athletes of all time going, hey, man, needed to cry. I needed to let it go and needed to give myself some credit I'm enough. Like I even sometimes, because I'm kind of like, you were very similar. That's why I think I'm growing to be so, fond of you is that we both have pretty masculine sides to us, but we also, whatever you want to call it, there's also sort of a, you can call it a feminine side, I guess. So, people call fem, if you show feelings, you're feminine, so, to speak, right? I don't have any problems saying that. And sometimes people will say to me, oh, I love when you don't tell people they're enough when they're not enough. And I'm like, no, they are enough.

Right. And if they don't believe they're enough, you're not going to get there. How much of it is about being present though? I would think when you have 100 days and I'm just spit balling here, cause you're the one who did it, but kind of down your road. The other thing that happens when we're down, or even when we're winning, we go, I'm going to have to do this 11 more times. I'm going to have to make phone calls 800 more days of my business career. I'm going to have to find 9,000 more clients. Like they start projecting further down the road and stacking this impossibility. When most things are in bite sized chunks in life, I didn't get to wherever I am. I certainly didn't end up, you know, ocean front of wherever it is like, because I projected forward. If you'd have told me everything I had to do to get here, I probably would not have started. But if you share what I got to do today, I'll do it today. Right? How much have I got to think with 100 of these? It's like, it might never be the day. It might just be the next step. I don't know. What it is, how to do it.

James Lawrence (00:28:43):

You do that? Yeah, for sure. You've got to break it down into really small, manageable chunks.

Are you, do you get overwhelmed? Um, and I actually call it catastrophe ism. And what that is, is looking into the future, um, in an event or a situation that hasn't happened yet and then continually feeding it and giving it energy until it blows out of proportion and control. And it engulfs you, consumes you and completely breaks you down and sidelines you. And that's what happens to all of us like guys business or whatever it is, your to-do list is never going to end. And so, like, stop trying to like worry about the pieces of the puzzle that you don't know. And, and that's another great point is like, you're not gonna know everything when you start. And so, stop worrying about it, but just you got to start and start executing.

And it was interesting. I had, I had an experience, um, it was deep into the campaign. Well, two experiences, there was somebody we ran on this, this, this asphalt trail by my house and early on somebody, I still don't know who it is. They wrote the words conquer 100 on the trail with spray paint. And then every single day when I would complete it, they would come out and put a hash mark. I was so, at this person, eight days in because every single time I would go buy it. And it was a reminder that I had 92 more to go. And I was like, are you freaking kidding me? Like stop doing whatever you're doing. I cannot, I cannot compartmentalize and figure out how to do 82 more of these, because I'm trying to be present, stop bringing to my attention that this is happening now.

I was grateful when they were like, there was a, you know, 90 something hash marks. And I'm like, yeah, there's 90 that each one of those represents something. And then they threw this party at 51 when we broke or officially broke the world record. And then we broke it every single day, but they were like, dude, you're halfway there. And I'm like, F you don't tell me I'm halfway there. Because that means to me, I still have halfway to go. Don't bring that to my consciousness. And, and it got to the point where I had to, I had to break things down into manageable, smaller numbers to where I didn't have 14 to go. I had nine to go till five to go, and I could manage those smaller compartments. And it was interesting. I got into, I was so, hyper-focused on the moment what we were doing.

And some, a guy said to me, I was on 91 and he said, dude, you're so, close. You have nine more to go. And I looked at him and I said, no, I have three. And he goes, no, no, no, no, you have nine. And I looked at him and I said, you're a moron. I have three miles to go today. And I was so, focused on where I was right there in that moment. He was talking about full distance days to go. And I, I'm not even, I'm not even like my mind wasn't even, I could not comprehend what he was saying. And I'm like, you've been with me the whole marathon. How can you not know? We only have three to go. Why do you think we have nine? He was talking about days.

And I was so, present right there on the moment that I could not comprehend what he was saying, because I only had three miles to go to where I was enough that day. And so, you've gotta be on any journey that you on, whether it's lists or business or marriage or whatever, be there right now. I've got five kids and people always like, hey, you know, how do you do, how do you do family, balance and, and do what you do. And I'm like, it's not about 30%, 30%, 30%. My daughters they're teenage girls. They don't want 30% of my time. Kidding me. They want me to be all there for four minutes.

But when I'm there in those four minutes, I better be there with them for those four minutes. And so…

Ed Mylett ([00:32:35](00:32:35)):

James, I think you've hit on something brother, because I'm going to tell you the peak performers that I coach, you know, outside too, they have an ability to shrink timeframes. And so, they have a long-term plan. Like you set out conquer 100, that's the long-term vision. Most people can get backed up. They can go, I want a beach house. I want a dream relationship. I want 8% body fat. That's the big thing most people can get there. It's the day-to-day executing at a super high level, in a hyper focused, intentional state that most people don't have.

And it's because they're projecting into the future. And to some extent that projection into the future is a cop out distracting from your lack of execution right now, and the best pitchers aren't trying to throw a no-hitter, they're trying to execute this slider low and away. The Becks go, you know, this from golf, the best golfer. Isn't thinking about the 16th hole on hole three. They're thinking about this nine-iron to 1 46, 5 feet left of the hole in that shot.

James Lawrence (00:33:36):

We all the time, you have to have a short-term memory. You have to have short term memory and, and, and you have to have the vision for the long-term goal. But, um, and I'm totally going to botch the saying, I don't even know who said it, but like focus and intent right now today, we'll take care of the future and the long-term goal. You don't even have to worry about it. If you're executing with incredible focus and intent, now, everything else takes care of itself.

Ed Mylett (00:34:08):

All right. Who's the longest sponsor of this show. Omax cryo freeze. Why? Because the product is amazeballs have been using it now for almost two years. Why? Because if you have any pain, any discomfort, any soreness you need cryo freeze. The product was kind of modeled initially after like cryotherapy in a bottle. I use it after I work out, I use the one before I work out. Oftentimes I'll put it on before I go to bed at night, even just sitting around all day, right? You just get sore and achy and cryo freeze helps with the guys. It's just an awesome product. And if you have not tried it, try it because you're probably going to keep reordering it. It's made a huge difference for me.

And again, you guys all know this, my dad was using it up until, you know, when he passed away from cancer, my dad used it for his aches and pains and soreness because he was still working out even when he was sick. So, I'm a big believer in these guys and Omax is offering my listeners 20% off a one-month supply. So, right now, if you go to Omax health.com and enter the code, my let you get 20% off that's Omax health.com enter the code, my lab, which is M Y L E T T to get 20% off Omax trial, freeze and everything. Sitewise again, Omax health.com. Enter the code. My let get you 20% off back to the show.

Ed Mylett (00:35:19):

What about fear? So, because there's so, much brilliance, I've watched some of your talks. Obviously, I read the book, but you talk about, I'm gonna tell you something interesting about me that I'll share. I don't know if you have this or not, but I think if I think people, some people might be surprised to know that I'm, uh, I'm easily fearful.

What I mean by that is like, just because my upbringing, when I say fearful, meaning I can, my mind will find something to worry about if I let it. And, uh, and that's why I have to work on my mental toughness, because if I get mentally weak, my mental weakness for me, manifests in different people, mental weakness for me is that I'm going to quit, or I can't do this mental weakness for me manifest itself sometimes in anger and manifest itself sometimes in worry or fears. What if this happens and you talk about like isolating and attacking a fear. I forget where I saw you say or write this, but what do you mean by that? And how the heck do you do it? Yeah.

James Lawrence (00:36:11):

So to overcome, like, to me, fear is no different than like fear is just an emotion and feel like there's fear. There's, there's happiness, there's sadness, they're all, they're all just emotions. And we can, um, there's so, many tools and resources out there to overcome any of those buckets. Right? And, and the, the more we, the more we isolate ourselves and focus on something, the more it magnifies and becomes real.

And so, so, what people do is they have this fear, which is an irrational thought process because of either lack of preparation or experience. And so, when I said that, I meant, look, you've got to realize what your fear is. And then tack it with relentless pursuit and break it down into a manageable piece that you can go and then have confidence and momentum to take on the next piece of it.

Right. And so, it's just like we were talking about being present. Let's say our fear we'll compare that to the giant goal. Okay. You're not just going to rush and accomplish the big goal. You've got all of the tasks that are manageable along the way as you're present to try to get there fears. The same thing. If fear is the big goal, you don't have to break down that fear into something that is manageable and a little less scary to where you can go and take it on head on and fight that fight.

Now, as you gain momentum and experience, and you're getting closer to what the true root or true fear is now you're gaining momentum and confidence and having success along the way. By the time you get there, you've overcome it. And it's no longer a fear. And that's what people need to do is they need to show up in their lives, but they need to break things down to where you gain the success. You gain the momentum, and you can ultimately, you know, by the time you get there, you fit. You're, you're a prize fighter. And you're like, let, let, let's go. I'm gonna, I'm gonna, I'm going to drop, kick you in the face. I'm going to haul Kogan leg, drop you. And it's over.

Ed Mylett ([00:38:08](#)):

Somebody should be, uh, transcribing this and just turning it into a book on mental toughness and achievement seriously is what it should be. I just sitting here going, by the way, I love the hoaxster just so, you know, that's why I ate vitamins when I was a kid was because the whole Cogan. So, what about this? I'm going to ask you a couple of things. What's the hardest part about this? You just said, Hey man, the hardest part about conquer 100 endurance in general, the hardest part is, was what—

James Lawrence (00:38:38):

I think truly it, it's, it's believing in yourself that you can do it because it's, it's belief in conviction. It's getting to the point where you have the belief and conviction, where it's impossible for you to fail. And I listened to, um, the recently the, the podcast with Tim Grover and, and dude stud love his stuff, but I am going to disagree with something that he said. Um, and, and I believe he meant it to once you've reached this level and you want to win at the highest level, it's no longer I showed up and that's a success. And I, and I think for the masses showing up needs to be celebrated because they, they're so, lost. And this generation showing up is a problem. My daughter, my daughter is the,

the, the supervisor at her job. And, and this is going to blow your mind.

There's a three-strike policy on a no call, no show you're allowed to no call, no show three times before you're fired. Can you imagine an employer when you were working and growing up in fighting and digging? You don't even, it's like they don't even warn you when one, no call, no show. I'm sorry. You're gone. Right? The fact that in today's day and age, there is a three-strike policy on a no-call no-show completely blew my mind.

And so, I think I have a little bit of empathy for, this, I struggle understanding it because of the massive generation gap. My kids will call me a boomer, but, um, it's crazy that I fall into that category, but I do think showing up needs to be celebrated because that's where it starts. And a lot of times showing up is the hardest thing, because you're overwhelmed, you're daunted, and people don't have the confidence yet because they don't have the experience, brother.

Ed Mylett (00:40:44):

I think Warren is mental. The best ability is availability, right? And the other part of it is learning to play hurt, learning to play physically hurt, obviously in your case, but learning to play mentally hurts, showing up and playing when things are a mess at home, showing up and playing when there's no money in the bank. Because I don't think that I have a lot of superpowers, but one of them it's ironic that you said is I would get my up and I would get to the office when I didn't eat breakfast, because I had no money for breakfast kind of hope. And if I busted my butt that day, somebody at the office would take me to lunch. Right? That's the truth. And so, that shows up, but you look at right now, as we're recording this, the NBA playoffs are going on.

It's a process of attrition, frankly. I don't think the best team's going to win this year. The, the esteem is late. It's the Lakers. Maybe it might've been the nets, but they, they couldn't get guys to show up because they were hurt and they couldn't play hurt. There's a difference between injured and hurt. I get that. But the point I'm saying is this year, there's probably going to be a championship held up by somebody who's not the most talented, not the most gifted didn't have the best record during the season because they showed up. They couldn't get their bodies to show up. You're absolutely right about this.

James Lawrence (00:41:58):

Can you, can you imagine if the NBA finals this year ends up being Atlanta versus Phoenix? Who would have said, oh yeah, I'm going to put all my money on Atlanta, Phoenix in the finals. Like everybody wouldn't like, what are you crazy? That's like a, for sure way to flush your money down the toilet.

Ed Mylett (00:42:15):

Even if one of them, even if one of them gets in, that's amazing.

James Lawrence (00:42:17):

It's insane. And here here's, what's interesting about this concept is I got asked the question, hey, at what point in time during your day, do you know that you're going to finish? And I said, well, that's easy. As soon as I get in the water. Wow. And, and to me, that's where I think it's important to celebrate just showing up because in my world, when I show up, I know it's accomplished. I know it's done. And some triggers you to finish, that's showing up, triggers me to finish. And it creates that momentum going forward. So, really the answer to the question is when, at what point in time did you know you were going to be successful? And I said, well, as soon as I did the first stroke, and as soon as I made the decision to show up, I knew the goal was done because how many of us don't show up and don't have that clear path to what we're doing. So, for me, I celebrate showing up because in my mind showing up means I've completed the goal.

Ed Mylett (00:43:15):

Yep. And I think we both, I know exactly what you mean. And I know we both know what Tim was saying at the highest level is that there's a level passed out, but the baseline function to get into the pool of success, you have to be there swimming. Even if it's with floaties on, you've got to get there. Even if you're in the shallow end, you want to go play in the deep end. That's another story Grover's talking about. The deepest, deepest end, but just getting in that pool, the success pool is something to be celebrated. And for you, the trigger is I'm in the pool. I'm finishing.

James Lawrence (00:43:45):

I'm done. And I think, I think it's important for people to understand that you're never going to feel ready. And that's why it's important to show up. Because by showing up, you start to gain that knowledge and experience that you need in order to bridge that gap from where you were to where you're going. nobody shows up and is an expert. I have this picture of me and my very first event where I'm holding. It was in a pool I'm holding on to the edge of the pool, gasping for air, with a nose plug on, because I don't know how to, I don't know how to swim. And I promise you, nobody would have looked at that guy and said, he's going to go on and, and, and break for world records and set sports, endurance history. Nobody would like, that's just like saying Atlanta and Phoenix going to be in the finals.

Nobody puts their money on that guy. But that's my point. And I hope that people get from this is you need to show up when you're not ready. And when you don't have the confidence, because that's how you gain the confidence to be ready, to take it to another level so, that you don't have to celebrate showing up, like Grover saying, you can now focus on winning, right. And to where you can just, just consciously be conscious. And it like a full distance for me became routine to where my body craved doing it. And it became the new normal, what would have happened? Had I not decided to show up because I didn't feel I was ready. How many thousands of people around the world I've had has our family had an opportunity to impact? I can't tell you the, the messages that have come around the world of, of people.

I was out walking on the marathon. I can't remember what day it was. And a guy came up to me and he said, hey, you don't, you don't know me. Um, but, um, before the journey started, literally the day before the journey started, I almost took my own life. And he goes, I showed up on day one and I watched you. And I just, I just wanted to see what you were doing. And then I showed up on day number two. And by the time I hit day, number 10, I saw the intense struggle that you were going. And you set the example that you just have to keep showing up and face the demons and adversity and things can get easier. And he goes, you saved my life. Oh my gosh. And I can't tell you, we have 100 of those stories and I can't help but wonder what would've happened.

If I decided not to show up when I didn't think I was worthy or had value to show up and start my journey, because we truly have no idea. Who's watching, especially as a parent, I mean our kids, holy cow, they are watching the, hear everything. They see everything. They, they may tell you, they hate you, but you are their hero. And I think as adults, we need to, we have a responsibility to be the, be the best who we are at all times, because we have no idea who's watching.

And I think our kids are watching, even when we think we're alone and it's the most impactful times of our lives. And I think who we are when we think nobody's watching is who we truly are to our core and what our values truly are. And so, I think we need to do a constant self-audit of who we are in those moments when nobody's watching, because that's who our true character is. And I believe what our potential is. And so, if we can be extraordinary and spectacular in the dark, when we think nobody's watching, imagine what you can do when the lights are on and you, and you have thousands of people watching you. Imagine the impact that you can have on individuals if you were to show up in your life with that type of intent every single day, the, the legacy that you could leave, if that's who you were on a, on a 24-hour basis.

Ed Mylett (00:47:34):

All right. So, you entrepreneurs that are listening today. If you're still like doing QuickBooks and all that stuff, it's like quicksand for an entrepreneur, the bigger your company grows, the faster you sync with outdated software. So, the up-to-date modern way to do this stuff. I'm just going to tell you straight up is net suite, net suite is by Oracle. So, it's a huge backed company. It's a scalable solution. Run all of your key back-office stuff. No matter how big or small your company is, that's suite gives you visibility and control over your financials, inventory, HR. E-commerce literally everything in one spot, one click. It's not expensive. It's totally worth it. I think you should look into it for sure. Helps you automate your key business processes, close your books, and about a fraction of the time. In fact, 93% of the companies surveyed increased visibility and control over their businesses since making the switch from QuickBooks to NetSuite.

So right now, NetSuite's offering a one-of-a-kind financing program only for those ready to graduate from QuickBooks. So, head to netsuite.com/mylett, there's special financing for you guys there. Netsuite.com/mylett. And again, it's M Y L E T T, go there. Now, netsuite.com/mylett. Let's get back after it.

Ed Mylett (00:47:34):

It's just so, good. I, uh, you said earlier that fear is an emotion. One of these things about kids, I would just add that. You're saying our kids are watching everything. And I used to think your kids are going to behave just like you behave. That's not always true. Some do some don't that they're going to think, just like you think some do some don't me tell you what I think most kids end up mirroring as they become adults, your emotions. So, if they see you live with a particular set of emotions, anger, fear, worry, depression, their life may go out and they may produce external results, but they'll find themselves their emotional home being those same emotions they saw you experiencing. And so, but if they see you experiencing joy, ecstasy, passion, triumph, challenge, you know, these other emotions, they do mirror mode.

I found that, you know, my dad's life was very different than mine, right? He, you know, that he had drank and all that. But as I got older, I was, I behaved a little bit like my dad, but I did sort of experience the same emotions as him, even though our external lives are very different. Some of those emotions I wanted to have, because I loved my dad, but some of them I didn't. And I'm like, why am I not happier? Why am I down? When I've got all this stuff? I learned to embody those emotions, watching my dad all those years. And so, you listening to this, what emotions do you carry that to your parents and in front of your children? What emotions are they seeing you experience? Because they see you in the quiet times, they see you driving in the car, they see you when you get home from work and it's all right.

They see those things. And so, be cognizant of your emotion. Speaking of emotions, I got to think to do something. This is again, we've got a couple more minutes. Thank you for today. By the end. I mean, that's someone transcribe this, put it in a book and sell the heck out of it. But, um, what about your reasons? I say, I think big goals are awesome, but when I meet people that have deep emotional reasons for doing this or whatever it is they're doing that typically overrides most pain, most fear, most adversity when they can reflect on those reasons, what are yours. And is there any time during these 100 days that you reflect on it either during the running swimming or biking or when you're resting in the evening?

James Lawrence (00:50:51):

I think the number one reason people fail in anything that they're doing is because of the reason the benefit, the value didn't match, the sacrifice that they were doing. And I think that is the reason why most people fail is because they haven't put enough thought and time into what they're doing. And I call it a bag of whys. And everybody says, what's your why? What's your reason? And I promise you, if you go into a journey that has meaning that is going to push you to the brink, that is going to challenge you to your very core, it's going to back you into a corner and you're going to experience some darkness that you've never felt. I promise you, your one reason is not enough. And you're going to have to pull all of the reasons and put them together into one big ball of purpose and reason in order to overcome that moment, because you're going to get there and you're going to go, this is why I started now that I'm in the pain that I'm in and I'm backed into the corner.

Ah, that's not enough and I'm out. And so, so, if you're on the cusp of something big and on a journey. I think it's super important to sit back and reflect and start to compile the reasons that that you're doing it. And it can't be a lifetime reason, right? Things are always going to evolve and change. When I was on the 50, we had lost everything. We were broke. I wasn't financially stable. We had lost our home. They had taken away from me and while I was out there, my reason was I'm going to take my life back. I'm going to build my dream home. And my I'm going to give my wife and kids, the family that I believe they deserve. Well, I had done that and going into the hundred that can no longer be my reason it has to change. And so, you have to be thoughtful and with intent, with the purpose and reason, you're doing things.

And to be honest with you, a huge reason for me on the hundred was because I said I would. And, and to me, even in the darkest of moments, my word meant so much that I could not set that ultimate example for my kids and watch them or have them watch me back out for really no good reason, pain, discomfort, just because I'm done. And to me showing my kids that ultimate example of you, you say you're going to do something which think is a lost art to me. When I said I was going to do it, it was my virtual handshake to anybody that was listening, that I'm committing to do that. And I, and I think the day and age of like, there's gotta be an ironclad contract and this money on the line and that my, no, I shook your hand.

And I said, I'm going to go out and do the Conquer 100 project. And to me it was, I'm going to prove to everybody. But most importantly, myself and my family, that I am who I said I am. And without question, it's going to take hell or high water for me not to continue on the journey and to do what I said I was going to do. And to me, that was reason enough. And it should be reason enough for most people that our words should be our bond and integrity at the highest level should be the most important thing.

If you lead with love and integrity, the cream will always rise to the top. And sometimes it's going to take a little bit longer, but if you always strive to take the higher road, you never have to look over your shoulder. You never have to worry about somebody opening up the closet. You never have to worry about somebody else's opinion of you. You never have to worry about the journey that you're on because you have built that confidence of love and integrity, and you can go forward with intense confidence that no matter it doesn't matter what anybody else's opinion is because I have that love and integrity on the journey that I am. And my family served with me, and nothing can trump that.

Ed Mylett (00:54:54):

Brother, uh, you know, there's, there's people who say inspiring things and then there's inspiring people rarely or is somebody both. And it's, you're, you're incredible. Like I'm watching my face in the cameras. You're talking like I need to maintain my face. Cause you know, I don't, I've not only ever done that in an interview before. I got a lot of things I wanted to get to we'll have you back because you're incredible. But I do want to go through two more things. One was the hardest part, the lack of rest. I'm just curious because there's not a ton of rest. I mean, actual sleep. Like I was reading that you actually didn't just black out, but like you could fall asleep riding the bike true or false. True.

James Lawrence (00:55:39):

Um, so, let me contrast really quick, the difference between the 50 campaigns where we did 50 fulls and 50 days or 50 states. Yeah. And then the hundred where it was in a remote location

Ed Mylett (00:55:51):

And more rest than right. The second time. Correct.

James Lawrence (00:55:54):

So, so, if I was to pigeonhole or label the 50, it was, um, logistics, it was fatigue and it was chaos and then the hundred would have been pain and duration. Right. And so, so, the whole reason I believed that 100 was possible was if remove chaos, put systems in place, can we double what everybody thought was impossible and defy and defy logic. Right. And what happened was, is the chaos still ensued because you just can't predict the unpredictable. And when you're doing anything for a quarter of a year, you've, we've all heard that in order to achieve success, you've got to have it's when preparation meets luck and, and a lot of luck has to go into these types of things when you're doing it for that long. And so, to compare those two, um, the 100 was, was very difficult because of how long it was. And the, I mean, you're talking about going from 7,000-mile campaign to 14,000 miles, which is that compounding effect of that is super hard to, to rationalize it in our minds and in our, in our heads. And so, that, that's how I would compare the, the 50 and the 100.

Ed Mylett (00:57:22):

It's even as you say it, it's just, it's just unbelievable. It's just unbelievable. It's just, it's gotta be one step in front of the next. All right. Last question, by the way. Thank you for today. I know it goes without saying, like, I already know what the response is going to be to this. I have, you know, when I do interviews, I love all of them. Um, I won't have someone on my program anymore. We're lucky that we can get who we want, typically that I'm already not friends with fascinated by or inspired by or want to learn myself from. But then there are certain ones that I'm, I'm doing the conversation I'm in the interview. And, but I'm, I'm making decisions as you're talking, I'm making decisions as you're talking, man. And that's when I know it's profound and that's what I've been doing the whole time we're talking, share with us what it's like to finish to achieve it. So, you've had a few of these, you know, we're all sitting out here. Like I got my dream too, man, mine, isn't 100 conquer, 100, you know, it's not that my dream is X or Y what's it feel like I did it. What's that feeling like if you can even begin to describe it. Yeah.

James Lawrence (00:58:26):

This is, this could be an entire podcast to unpack because coming off the 50, they, I got heavily warned. They said, look, you're gonna fall into depression. You're gonna, um, have confusion, brain fog. You're not going to know what's, what's up. And I didn't experience that on the 50. And so, when I was coming off of the 100, was like, it's not going to happen. I've got this. I'm a man. I'm invincible. I just, I just, I just did sports history. I'm good. And, and I, you saw the emotion of crossing the finish line of the 100 and it was, that was raw. And that was real. And what I didn't expect was the depression, the confusion, the brain fog. I don't know when it happened, but at some point in the time I transitioned into a state to where I was in such trauma and turmoil that my brain was protecting me.

And it was not allowing me to feel. And I believe I was. And I, it was probably around 85 that now looking back on it, I was in the ultimate of flow state. And that's when it was, it was somebody said, the documentary asked me a question. I was on the table and they said, how many could you do? And I said, 200. I get didn't even hesitate. I was like 200. I was in such a state of like power and flow. And then I came out of it and I had this, like my brain and our brains are so, powerful ed, that it was masking every emotion that was real and that I was feeling. And, and it's, it's hard to explain, but I was in an ultimate protective state from trauma. And I now have a lot of empathy for people that are going through something intense that they aren't themselves, because they're trying to protect themselves from the feelings or the emotions or the trauma of what they're going through.

And I, and I would have never said I was in that state until I had an opportunity to come out of it. And it's been really hard. I've been walking around the house. I'm supposed to be recovering. I don't know what to do. That was who I, who I was. And that's who I, that was my identity and everything. And now that gets stripped away. And then you start questioning, well, who am I? Is that, is that my only value is that my only worth? And then now you start to have this like real conversation with yourself, okay. Now, where, what is my place? And you, you start to go this through this transitional conversation with yourself. And I think there's three phases to any big journey. It's preparation, it's execution. And then it's post and recovery to whatever that looks like. And I think we have to respect all three levels of that type of journey.

And the recovery portion of it could be the most important because it's when you unpack the lessons and you try to internalize the experience so, that you can evolve again and be a better person to have influence that you want to have to help other people have that same type of experience in their lives on a positive level. And so, I'm, again, I'm grateful for the struggle. I'm grateful for the lessons that I can learn so, that I can develop empathy for others that are in that situation. Um, and so, like we talked about I'm, I'm grateful for rock bottom. I'm grateful for the struggle. I'm grateful for the opportunity to learn those lessons so, that I can be a better father and person

Ed Mylett (01:02:09):

I'm grateful for you today. And hopefully it will Dawn on you when we finish this, that one of the places you belong is doing what we just did here today is literally the millions of people are affected by this, especially on the audio side, millions of people. And there were no wasted words today and only you are qualified to deliver these because of what you've gone through because of what you've achieved. Only you, no one else could do what you did today, because someone else has not gone down, literally the road that you've gone down, it makes me emotional to say. And so, it will begin to reveal itself to you brother, as you move forward, you're in that repair and recover stage. One of the real estate answers of all time, I've had the same sense. A lot of athletes, a lot of businesspeople have had those things happen.

Oftentimes mothers have it when they have the dream of giving childbirth. Now some of that is obviously chemical, but it is a thing that sometimes when this is, this journey ends, our identity changes the chemistry in our body. Isn't just right. And there's just, what's next? Is there a next, what's my value, all those things you said, I can just tell you that for everyone that listened to watch this today, they would all come back and she'd put their arms around. You hug, you go, brother, you just did it. You just spent an hour doing it. And then I could see the emotion on your face now. And so, little, did you know, it's the ripple effect. You know, only you are capable of delivering the words and the messages and the insights you have because only you have gone down that road. So, I'm grateful for you and a wow. Like just a wow. So, thank you. And I'm here to help you, by the way, you know that we've got each other's numbers, anything I can do in this transitional phase for you. Can I wrap up with one, one thought 100 percent? Yes.

James Lawrence (01:03:45):

Okay. So, I, I, I, I don't know if you tuned out after day 100. Um, do you know what we did the next day? No, I don't. Okay. So, um, we did 1 0 1. Did you really? And, um, yeah, so, we went live every day during the swim and, and I, I think this is important because of who you are and, you know, your tagline of, uh, max out.

And, and we turned on the live the following day when I would have normally been swimming every single day. And it was, and it was just me in the pool by myself, doing one more. And I got asked the question a lot. Why did you do one more? And I had a lot of people understand, and then I had a lot of people, just, they were confused. And I hate the cause. My, the way I feed my family is I get on stage and we tell our story.

We, we motivate, and we do coaching and, whatnot. Um, and I, and I love, talking from stage and impacting people. Um, and, and I don't appreciate the speakers that are out there telling, uh, trying to teach a lesson when they haven't done it. They haven't been on the battlefield in the battle. And I felt like I would be a hypocrite if I told people that you can up and you can do one more. And it, the campaign they, 100 was on a Tuesday and Sunday night, I said, I just got the most intense impression, James, you need to do one more. And I was like, are you freaking kidding me? Like, I am broken. Like I am mentally exhausted. I've been showing up for a quarter of a year. Why would I do one more? And they, and I got the impression it's not for you.

And, and I felt like our team needed to show up and do one more because on your journey, when you're broken and when you are at your limit, I promise you, you can get up and you can do one more. And that one more might be by yourself. And I don't know how many times you're going to have to get up and do one more by yourself, but I promise you, you can get up one more. And I didn't feel like I, I could bring integrity to our story if I didn't go out. And as a team, we did one more. And so, we did, we did 1 0 1 because I, I want to lead from the front. And I want to show people when you are broken. And when you have reached your limit, you can do one more.

Ed Mylett (01:06:40):

James, that book I'm writing right now is called One More.

James Lawrence (01:06:44):

You just stole the title of my next book, Ed, we're in a fight, right.

Ed Mylett (01:06:48):

Might be out before you. Yeah. And I'm adding your story to the book because I have the rights to this podcast, but I'm not exaggerating. I'm almost done. And I told you that you went on this journey. You did this, I know you did it from audience, but you just did it for me. And, so, I'm sure the books will be very different in content. But yeah, the, my book is the power of one more and it'll be out in the fall. And I'm so, excited for that book yet.

I'm just blown away that you just said that that may be the craziest thing that's ever been done on the show. And it was at the end. I hope everyone's still listening. Cause that's a, that's a wow, thank God you added that to unbelievable conversation. So, thank you, James. Everybody go find, find the Iron Cowboy on Instagram, follow him, get his book, book him to speak. It's just, he's the real deal.

Like he said, like you're bringing someone in, who's done these things and does not struggle through the ability to articulate his thoughts and his points and his emotions. He's got an anointing with his language as well. So, thank you for today, brother—and everybody out there, share this and subscribe. If you're listening to the audio, subscribe to YouTube. If you're watching YouTube, go subscribe to Stitcher, Spotify, or iTunes, or one of these platforms, get the audio version as well. God bless you all, max out.

Announcer (01:08:08):

This is the Ed Mylett show.

Printed in Great Britain
by Amazon